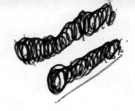

AN INTRODUCTION
TO
SCORE PLAYING

BY

ERIC TAYLOR

OXFORD   NEW YORK
OXFORD UNIVERSITY PRESS

Oxford University Press, Walton Street, Oxford OX2 6DP
Oxford New York Toronto
Delhi Bombay Calcutta Madras Karachi
Petaling Jaya Singapore Hong Kong Tokyo
Nairobi Dar es Salaam Cape Town
Melbourne Auckland
and associated companies in
Beirut Berlin Ibadan Nicosia

Oxford is a trade mark of Oxford University Press

© Oxford University Press 1970

First published 1970
Reprinted 1984, 1986, and 1987

ISBN 0–19–321731–7

Acknowledgements are due to the following for permission to use music
extracts: MM. Durand & Cie, Editeurs-Propriétaires, Paris (Ravel: Ma
mère l'oye); Novello & Co. Ltd. (Bliss: Clarinet Quintet; Elgar Wand of
Youth Suites); and Schott & Co. Ltd. (Hindemith: Sonate für vier
Hörner).

Printed in Great Britain by
J. W. Arrowsmith Ltd, Bristol

Preface

An earlier collection of score-reading exercises, *Playing from an Orchestral Score*, was intended for use mainly by students in the third year of a university or conservatoire course. This new book has been compiled in response to requests for material to use at an earlier stage. It is not, however, simply a collection of rather easier passages. *Playing from an Orchestral Score* dealt from the beginning with the problems of arrangement, problems which are inescapable when one tries to represent orchestral music on the piano. The present exercises avoid the need for arrangement; indeed they have been chosen precisely because, with an occasional awkward stretch, the pianist can play every written note. An exact literal performance must be the intention: any less thorough approach will fail to produce the facility in grasping detail which is essential to the performance of more complex passages—especially those requiring arrangement.

It is only in double bass parts that there may be exceptions to the general rule that all notes sounded by the various instruments must be reproduced on the piano. Account should always be taken, of course, of the true pitch (an octave below the written notes) of the double bass, most especially where it has an independent line (e.g. Ex. 33). Even where the written notes on the double bass are the same as those of the cello its sounding notes should be played wherever possible. Example 9, for example, starts:

Nevertheless, in the later examples, especially in Part II, the octaves are not always practically possible. In these cases no damage is done if the double bass notes are omitted, either in part or *in toto,* provided the performer is clear what is happening.

The exercises have been arranged in two parts. Part I is further subdivided into three sections: Section A provides practice in reading the alto clef; Section B introduces the two related problems of the tenor clef

and transposing parts in B flat (related because ![notation example showing tenor clef note equals treble clef note in B♭, 8va bassa])

and Section C adds other common transpositions—in order of difficulty rather than of frequency. Thus horns in E flat appear first (because

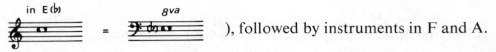), followed by instruments in F and A.

Part II is not arranged so systematically, and there is no reason why some of its examples should not be studied concurrently with those in Part I. It consists entirely of orchestral excerpts, all of which can be played virtually exactly on the piano. Such passages are not easy to find, but they provide a logical introduction to the more typical material in *Playing from an Orchestral Score*.

Apart from the alternative bass notes in Ex. 3 and the deletion of some blank staves the examples have not been altered or edited. Bar numbers have been added to show the position of each passage in the original work. I have again made no attempt to be consistent in the nomenclature of instruments: it is clearly necessary that they should be recognised in more than one language. Since it may be helpful to refer to it, the Table of Instruments in *Playing from an Orchestral Score* has been reproduced on pp.8-9.

I think many who use this book will be interested to learn that all the music examples (like those in *Playing from an Orchestral Score*) were drawn by Mr. Jonathan Barkwith: they are not the result of any typesetting process. I am very grateful to him for his beautiful work.

E.T.

CONTENTS

*Bar numbers have been added to show where each extract occurs in the original work.

TABLE OF INSTRUMENTS

English[1]	Italian	German	French	Transposition (if any)
flute	flauto, or flauto grande	Flöte, or grosse Flöte	flûte, or grande flûte	
piccolo	flauto piccolo, or ottavino	kleine Flöte	petite flûte	*(musical notation, 2)*
alto flute, or bass flute, or flute in G	flauto contralto	Altflöte	flûte en sol	*(musical notation)*
oboe	oboe	Oboe, or Hoboe	hautbois	*(musical notation)*
cor anglais, or English horn	corno inglese	englisch Horn	cor anglais	*(musical notation)*
oboe d'amore	oboe d'amore	Oboe d'amore or Liebesoboe	hautbois d'amour	*(musical notation)*
clarinet in B♭	clarinetto in si bemolle	Klarinette in B	clarinette en si bémol	in B♭
in A	in la	in A	en la	in A
in E♭	in mi bemolle	in Es	en mi bémol	in E♭
in D	in re	in D	en ré	in D
bass clarinet	clarinetto basso or clarone	Bassklarinette	clarinette basse	*(musical notation, German notation / French notation)*
bassoon	fagotto	Fagott	basson	
double bassoon or contrabassoon	contrafagotto	Kontrafagott	contrebasson	*(musical notation)*
horn, or French horn	corno	Horn (pl.[3] Hörner)	cor	
natural horn	corno naturale	Waldhorn	cor simple	
valve horn	corno ventile, or corno cromatico	Ventilhorn	cor à pistons, or cor chromatique	*(musical notation)[4]*
in B♭	in si bemolle	in B	en si bémol	in B♭ alto
in A	in la	in A	en la	in A
in A♭	in la bemolle	in As	en la bémol	in A♭
in G	in sol	in G	en sol	in G

Transposition labels (with musical staves):
in F · in E · in Eb · in D · in C · in Bb · basso · in A
in F · in E · in D · in C · in Bb · in A
in F · in Bb · in A

English	Italian	German	French
in F	in fa	in F	en fa
in E	in mi	in E	en mi
in Eb	in mi bemolle	in Es	en mi bémol
in D	in re	in D	en ré
in C	in do	in C	en ut
trumpet	tromba (pl. trombe)	Trompete	trompette 
cornet	cornetta	Kornett	cornet à pistons 
trombone	trombone (pl. tromboni)	Posaune	trombone
tuba	tuba	Tuba	tuba
kettle drums	timpani	Pauken	timbales
side drum, or snare drum	tamburo piccolo, or tamburo militare	kleine Trommel	caisse claire, or tambour militaire
bass drum	cassa, or gran cassa	grosse Trommel	grosse caisse
cymbals	piatti, or cinelli	Becken	cymbales
gong	tam-tam	Tam-tam	tam-tam
triangle	triangolo	Triangel	triangle
bells	campane	Glocken	cloches
glockenspiel	campanelli	Glockenspiel	jeu de timbres, or carillon
xylophone	xilofono, or silofono	Xylophon	xylophone
harp	arpa	Harfe	harpe
violin	violino	Violine	violon
viola	viola	Bratsche	alto
cello	violoncello	Violoncell	violoncelle 
double bass, or bass	contrabasso, or basso	Kontrabass	contrebasse 

1. The 'English' terms given are those generally accepted in modern usage, even though they are in some cases foreign words.
2. The note in brackets is always the *written* note. It is followed by the note which is actually sounded (i.e. the 'concert' note). The key-signatures of all transposing parts must, of course, be adjusted, with one exception: horn parts are written without key-signatures at all times, with necessary accidentals added throughout. Modern composers occasionally give the horns a key-signature, but this is not the standard practice.
3. Plurals are usually clear enough, but I have given them in a few cases where they are a little less obvious or where there may be confusion: 'trombe', for example, is *not* a contraction for trombone!
4. Note that in the treble clef the horn *always* sounds lower than written. When a horn in C, therefore, sounds an octave lower than written. When a horn uses the bass clef it is customarily written an octave lower than it would otherwise have been, e.g.:

in F

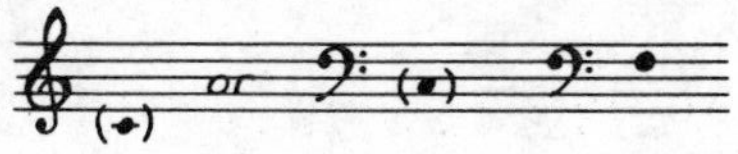

5. Composers who do not observe this illogical convention are usually wise enough to draw attention to the fact in a footnote. (See also footnote 2).
5. Contemporary composers usually write cello parts at the pitch of their actual sounds throughout. Formerly it was the practice to write parts an octave too high where they used the treble clef, unless a passage in the tenor clef preceded the treble clef.

Part I

Section A

1

Printed in Great Britain
OXFORD UNIVERSITY PRESS, MUSIC DEPARTMENT, WALTON STREET, OXFORD OX2 6DP

2

3

TRIO I (Allegretto)

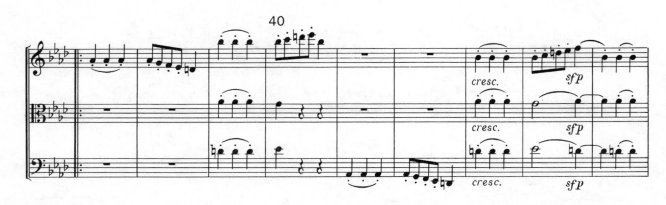

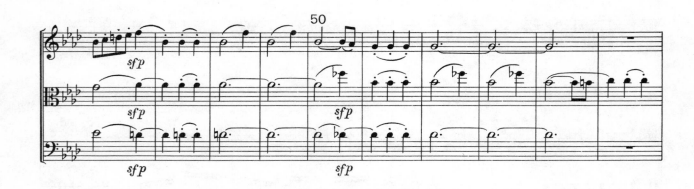

The bracketed cello notes are alternatives suggested for ease of performance.

4

5

Poco allegretto e grazioso

* *(Actual sounds)*

14

6

Andante (quasi Allegretto)

7

8

Andante con moto

9

10

11

12

Largo cantabile

Fagotto

Violino I

Violino II

Viola

Violoncello e Basso

13

* (Actual sounds. The passage was originally written an octave higher.)

14

15

16

17

18

19

20

21

31

22

Andante un poco moto

23

Lento assai, cantante e tranquillo

24

25

35

26

Menuetto I

27

Allegro con spirito

28

29

30

31

40

34

35

36

47

37

38

39

40

41

(**Allegretto** ♪= 120)

60

Part II

42

43

44

45

48

49

Can be read as though in the alto clef.

51

52

53

54

73

55

56

57

76

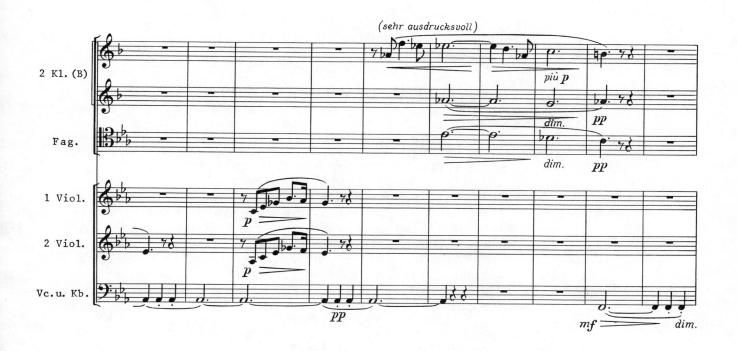

Reproduced and printed by
Halstan & Co. Ltd., Amersham, Bucks., England

INDEX OF WORKS